Religions Today

Sikhism

Jon Mayled

Heinemann
LIBRARY

www.heinemann.co.uk/library
Visit our website to find out more information about **Heinemann Library** books.

To order:
☎ Phone 44 (0) 1865 888066
▤ Send a fax to 44 (0) 1865 314091
▣ Visit the Heinemann Bookshop at www.heinemann.co.uk/library to browse our catalogue and order online.

Heinemann Library
Halley Court, Jordan Hill, Oxford, OX2 8EJ
Part of Harcourt Limited

Heinemann is the registered trademark of Harcourt Education Limited

Text © Jon Mayled, 2002

Original illustrations © Heinemann Educational Publishers 2002

First published in 2002

ISBN 0 431 14976 3 (hardback)
05 04 03 02
10 9 8 7 6 5 4 3 2 1

ISBN 0 431 14983 6 (paperback)
06 05 04 03
10 9 8 7 6 5 4 3 2 1

British Library Cataloguing in Publication Data
A catalogue record for this book is available from the British Library

Picture research by Jennifer Johnson
Typeset by Artistix, Thame, Oxon
Illustrated by Artistix
Printed and bound in Spain by Edelvives

Acknowledgements
The publishers would like to thank the following for permission to use photographs:

The Environmental Picture Library/Graham Burns, p. 50; TRIP/H. Luther, pp. 45, 56; TRIP/Resource Foto, p. 48; TRIP/H. Rogers, pp. 2, 5, 6, 7, 8, 9, 10 (right), 12, 13, 19, 20 (both), 21, 23, 24, 25, 28, 29, 49, 52, 54, 55, 58, 59; Harjinder Singh Sagoo, pp. 3, 10 (left), 14, 15, 18, 26, 27, 30, 31, 32, 33, 34, 35, 36, 37, 38, 40, 41, 42, 43, 44, 46, 47, 53, 57; TRIP/R. Westlake, p. 51.

The publishers have made every effort to contact copyright holders. However, if any material has been incorrectly acknowledged, the publishers would be pleased to correct this at the earliest opportunity.

Websites
Links to appropriate websites are given throughout the pack. Although these were up-to-date at the time of writing, it is essential for teachers to preview these sites before using them with pupils. This will ensure that the web address (URL) is still accurate and the content is suitable for your needs. We suggest that you bookmark useful sites and consider enabling pupils to access them through the school intranet. We are bringing this to your attention as we are aware of legitimate sites being appropriated illegally by people wanting to distribute unsuitable and offensive material. We strongly advise you to purchase suitable screening software so that pupils are protected from unsuitable sites and their material. If you do find that the links given no longer work, or the content is unsuitable, please let us know. Details of changes will be posted on our website.

Contents

In this section you will:

- learn about and understand what faith and trust mean
- consider how Sikhism seeks to strengthen faith in Waheguru (God)
- think about the aims of Sikhism.

Faith and trust

The people who follow **Sikhism** are called Sikhs. The word 'Sikh' means a disciple, someone who follows the teachings of a leader. In Sikhism, these are the teachings of the **Gurus**.

All Sikhs have faith and trust in God, called **Waheguru** – Wonderful Lord, the God who created all things.

Like all other religions, Sikhism is based on a system of **beliefs**. Beliefs are things that people think to be true, even if there is little evidence to support the beliefs.

Believing in something means that a person has **faith** and **trust** in what they believe. Faith is a firm and honest belief, that goes beyond all else. Trust is the certainty that what a person believes is right, a complete confidence in something, or a certainty that we will not be let down. For example, we may trust our friends.

Sikhs believe that their religion is a complete way of life. They believe that God created all things, and also that God has given guidance to help all people to live good lives. So, to be a true Sikh means to accept God and to carry out God's will.

Sikhism teaches that no one is better than anyone else. One of the main aims of Sikhism is that there should be a united human society living together in peace and equality and following the teachings of God. In particular, Sikhs believe in **sewa** – selfless service for others.

Sikhism gives freedom of thought to all believers. It aims to help people reach **mukti**, so that they can escape from being reborn again and again. To reach mukti they must show love and obedience to God.

Poster showing the ten Gurus and the Guru Granth Sahib JI

Sikhism aims to free people from vanity and greed, from envy and tension, from fear and insecurity. Sikhism also aims to free people from the worship of false gods and low desires, and shows them the beautiful hope of goodness and excellence which leads to freedom. Sikhism fills the heart with love for God and for all God's creation.

Sikhs are certain of their faith because God has told people about Waheguru through the teachings of the Gurus.

The first of these Gurus was **Guru Nanak Dev Ji**. To show respect to the Gurus, Sikhs add the words Ji or Dev Ji, meaning 'Honoured Sir' to the names of the Gurus.

The word Guru has two syllables – the first, 'gu', means darkness and the second, 'ru', means light. A Guru is, therefore, someone who helps others pass from darkness to light.

Sikh women in the gurdwara

Truth and religion

There are different types of truth. Scientific truth is when an experiment can be repeated over and over again with the same results, to prove a truth. Historical truth is when there is evidence to prove that a particular event took place. Moral truth is the idea that people might 'know' what is right or wrong. Artistic truth is when a work of fiction appears to be 'true' to the way in which humans behave. Finally, there is religious truth. Religious people want to discover the truth which comes from God.

If we knew that the teachings of a religion were true, we would not just have to believe in a god because we would know, as a fact, that this god existed. When religious people say that they 'know' that their god exists, this is based on faith and belief. This makes the whole idea of religion different from any other sort of belief which people may have.

Guru Nanak Dev Ji 1

In this section you will:

● begin to learn about the Sikh Gurus

● find out about the early life and teachings of Guru Nanak Dev Ji.

Sikhism is the youngest of the six major world religions: Buddhism, Christianity, Hinduism, Islam and Judaism. It was founded by **Guru Nanak Dev Ji** in the fifteenth century.

The Sikh faith came from the teachings of the ten **Gurus**. They are all respected by Sikhs, but not worshipped because they were human beings, not gods.

Sikhs believe that the Gurus were all very special people who did not need to be reborn, but were sent back to earth to become God's messengers.

The Gurus taught that there is only one God, that all people are equally important before God and that everyone can attain **mukti** (freedom) if they live their lives with love and are faithful and obedient to God.

Guru Nanak Dev Ji's childhood

Guru Nanak Dev Ji was born in 1469 CE at Talwandi in the Punjab. Talwandi was later renamed Nankana Sahib in his honour and is now in Pakistan.

When he was born the astrologers said he would grow up to be someone special who would lead others towards God.

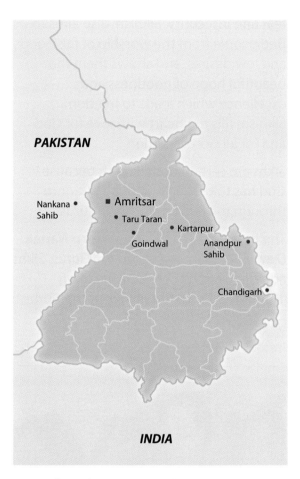

Map of north-west India showing the modern-day Punjab

Nanak's father, Mehta Kalu, was a Hindu and so brought up his son to follow this religion. When he was still young, Nanak did not accept the many rituals and customs of Hinduism.

When he was five years old he was sent to school. His teacher, Gopal Das, wrote the letters of the alphabet on a slate and Nanak asked what each letter meant. The teacher said that the letters themselves did not mean anything and asked Nanak what he thought the letters meant. Nanak went through the alphabet and used each letter as the start of a verse of poetry in praise of

God. This hymn can be read today in the Sikh scriptures, the **Guru Granth Sahib Ji**. The teacher realized that Nanak was no ordinary child, but a messenger of God.

When a Hindu boy reaches the age of about eleven years old he is given a sacred thread to wear. Nanak refused to wear it, saying that a thread could break, and what he wanted was 'that sacred thread which after the death of a man accompanies his soul to the next world'.

He said: 'Make kindness the material, and spin the thread of contentment. Tie knots of truth and virtue. These qualities in a person are the real sacred thread.'

On one occasion, Nanak's father sent him to a nearby town and gave him some money which he was told to spend wisely. On the way he met some holy men. He asked them how they could live without food, homes or jobs. The men told him that they had no need of these things because God provided for them. Nanak thought about this and when he arrived at the town he spent his money on food for the men.

When Nanak returned home his father was angry because he had intended that his son should invest the money not give it away.

An ordinary human

Sikhs show great honour and respect towards the person of Guru Nanak Dev Ji. Together with the other Gurus, he is given the title Dev Ji. Although he was the founder of Sikhism, he was an ordinary human being, and Sikhs do not believe that he was a god. Guru Nanak Dev Ji was a great leader, as was Muhammad (pbuh) in Islam. The earliest details we have about Guru Nanak Dev Ji come from Janam-Sakhis, or 'life stories', which were written between 50 and 80 years after his death.

Nanak was born in 1469. His father was a tax collector and a Hindu, belonging to the Kshatriya caste. Nanak's education was in Hinduism and Islam.

It is important to remember that Guru Nanak Dev Ji was born a Hindu and that it was his desire to bring together Hindus and Muslims that led to his seeking a new religion.

Guru Nanak Dev Ji – the first Guru

Guru Nanak Dev Ji 2

In this section you will:

● understand the importance of Guru Nanak Dev Ji's life and work

● consider Sikh teachings about equality

● read about Guru Nanak Dev Ji's travels.

One of the most important events in the life of **Guru Nanak Dev Ji** happened when he was 30 years old. Early every morning, Nanak went to the river to bathe and to pray. One day he did not return at his usual time. His friends went to the river and found his clothes on the bank, but there was no sign of Nanak. Three days later, he reappeared at the same place, but said nothing about what had happened to him.

This event had a great effect on his life. Guru Nanak Dev Ji left his home and family and travelled around the country teaching and preaching.

Guru Nanak Dev Ji taught that everyone should worship the same God and that every person was equal and should be treated equally. He said that there was 'no Hindu and no Muslim because everyone was equal in God's eyes'.

He said that people should always be prepared to work hard in order to serve God. He taught that human life is our chance to meet the creator, God, through having absolute love and devotion to **Waheguru**.

Guru Nanak Dev Ji also taught that arrogance, pride, lust, anger, greed and concerns about possessions all take us away from God.

Guru Nanak Dev Ji visited many holy Hindu places on his travels, including Varanasi in India

Guru Angad Dev Ji – the second Guru

He taught that rituals, idol worship, prejudice about people's **caste** (the belief that people are born into different groups), and any type of oppression, including the oppression of women, was wrong.

In 1520 CE Guru Nanak Dev Ji went to live in the village of Kartarpur in the Punjab and here he set up the first Sikh community.

A man called Bhai Lehna was making a pilgrimage to a Hindu shrine when he met Guru Nanak Dev Ji.

Lehna decided to visit Guru Nanak Dev Ji. He was wearing his best clothes. The people were gathering grass in the fields and there was one muddy bundle left. Lehna carried it to the village. Guru Nanak Dev Ji's wife was horrified to see the visitor carrying the bundle, but Guru Nanak Dev Ji told her that it was not a bundle of grass but 'a crown to honour the best of men'.

After this, Lehna served Guru Nanak Dev Ji in every way he could. Guru Nanak Dev Ji found Lehna to be the 'purest of the pure', and chose him above his own two sons.

He blessed Lehna, giving him the name Angad, which means 'part of me'. Bhai Lehna was now known as Guru Angad Dev Ji, the second Guru.

Teachings and travel

After leaving school, Guru Nanak Dev Ji worked as an accountant for an Afghan chieftain at Sultanpur. He composed hymns, and a Muslim servant, called Mardana, who played the rebec (a stringed instrument with a bow), set them to music.

While he was in Sultanpur Nanak with Mardana, Guru Nanak Dev Ji set up a kitchen where everyone could eat, whether they were Muslim or Hindu. This was the beginning of the **langar**.

Sikh tradition says that Nanak went on four long journeys. He travelled east to Assam; south to Ceylon (Sri Lanka); north to Ladakh and Tibet; and west to Makkah, al-Madinah and Baghdad.

Guru Nanak Dev Ji's teachings were that everyone was equal, and that everyone should be prepared to work hard in order to serve God. He said that human life gave people the chance to prove themselves worthy to meet God and to achieve **mukti**. Although he believed in reincarnation and the cycle of life and death, he rejected many of the teachings of Hinduism, including the caste system.

The Gurus 1

In this section you will:
- learn about the lives and teachings of some of the other Sikh Gurus
- gain an understanding of how they developed Sikhism.

Below we look at the four **Gurus** who followed **Guru Nanak Dev Ji**.

Guru Angad Dev Ji (1539–52)

Guru Angad Dev Ji collected together all the hymns of Guru Nanak Dev Ji and wrote them down, along with some of his own, in the **Gurmukhi** script.

Guru Angad Dev Ji encouraged Sikhs to take part in sport regularly. He believed that a healthy body and a healthy mind were both important to God.

Guru Amar Das Ji (1552–74)

Bhai Amar Das was 60 years old when he met Guru Angad Dev Ji. He was a Hindu, but the teachings in the Guru's **shabads** (hymns) made him see that God could only be served through true devotion and love and so he changed his whole way of life. He served Guru Angad Dev Ji for thirteen years.

Every day he collected water from the River Beas for the Guru's bath.

Guru Amar Das Ji became Guru when he was 73 years old. He encouraged the use of the **langar**, or Guru's kitchen, to carry on Guru Nanak Dev Ji's idea of communal eating. He also asked his followers to come to his headquarters in **Goindwal** three times a year on the dates of important Hindu festivals.

Guru Ram Das Ji (1574–81)

Guru Ram Das Ji founded the sacred city of **Amritsar**. He was the son-in-law of Guru Amar Das Ji, and took over from him in 1574 CE at the age of 40. Guru Ram Das Ji invited people from 52 different trades to come to Amritsar and start new businesses in the 'Guru's Market'. He also composed the **Lavan**, which is a special hymn sung at Sikh weddings. He died at the age of 57.

Guru Arjan Dev Ji (1581–1606)

Guru Arjan Dev Ji was the fifth Guru, and the youngest son of Guru Ram Das Ji.

The Golden Temple at Amritsar

and peaceful to show that all people should happily accept the will of God. Before his death, Guru Arjan Dev Ji sent a message that his son Har Gobind was to become the sixth Guru. He said that, because peaceful means had failed with the emperor, it was now right to use the sword to protect the weak and innocent.

Guru Arjan Dev Ji

Guru Arjan Dev Ji built the **Harimandir Sahib** (the Golden Temple) at Amritsar.

Guru Arjan Dev Ji collected the hymns of the first four Gurus, together with some of his own, in a volume called the **Adi Granth**. Once the Adi Granth was completed and placed in the Harimandir Sahib, Guru Arjan Dev Ji slept on the floor of the temple to show his respect for the word of God.

Guru Arjan Dev Ji was the first Sikh martyr. The Mogul emperor was jealous of the Guru and tried to convert Guru Arjan Dev Ji to Islam under the threat of death.

Guru Arjan Dev Ji refused and was tortured and killed. The torture lasted for five days. The Guru was placed in a tank of boiling water. The next day, he had to sit on a plate of red-hot iron. On the third day, red-hot sand was poured over his body. Guru Arjan Dev Ji remained calm

Developing Sikhism

These four Gurus are remembered because of the contributions they made towards the development of Sikhism.

Guru Angad Dev Ji began the collection of hymns which would later form the **Guru Granth Sahib Ji**. After the death of Guru Angad Dev Ji, all the Gurus who followed were from the Sodhi family of Guru Amar Das Ji.

Guru Amar Das Ji strengthened Guru Nanak Dev Ji's teaching about the langar.

Guru Ram Das Ji founded the city of Amritsar and composed the Lavan – the wedding hymn.

Guru Arjan Dev Ji (1581–1606) extended the collection of hymns begun by Guru Angad Dev Ji. He was the first Sikh martyr. Guru Arjan Dev Ji was also responsible for building the Harimandir in Amritsar, in 1604 CE. He designed the temple so that everyone had to step down to enter it, and with entrances on all four sides to show that it was open to all people. The foundation stone was laid by a Muslim holy man called Mian Mir.

The Gurus 2

In this section you will:

● learn about the lives and teachings of some more of the Sikh Gurus

● gain an understanding of how they developed Sikhism.

Below we look at the four **Gurus** who followed Guru Arjan Dev Ji.

Guru Har Gobind Ji (1606–44)

Guru Har Gobind Ji was the only son of Guru Arjan Dev Ji. He was eleven years old when his father was executed and he became the sixth Guru.

Guru Har Gobind Ji is sometimes called the 'Warrior Guru' because, after his father's death, he wore two **kirpans** (swords). One sword represented spiritual power, and the other, worldly power. These two swords appeared on the flags of his army and are now on the Sikh flag, the **Nishan Sahib**.

Guru Har Gobind Ji trained Sikhs to fight in order to defend themselves.

Even today, some Sikhs in India still wear 'warrior uniform'.

Guru Har Rai Ji (1644–61)

Guru Har Rai Ji was fourteen years old when he became the seventh Guru. His father instructed him that he should always have 2200 soldiers and horses with him.

Sikhs holding the Nishan Sahib

Guru Har Rai Ji

Guru Har Rai Ji set up a system so that free medicines were given to those who were sick. Today, some **gurdwaras** in India still give free medical treatment to the poor.

The emperor of India asked Guru Har Rai Ji to explain his hymns. He sent his son, Ram Rai, instead, telling him that not one word of the hymns could be changed because they were the words of God. Ram Rai broke the rules which his father had given him and so Guru Har Rai Ji declared that the next Guru would be his youngest son, Har Krishan.

Guru Har Krishan Ji (1661–64)

Guru Har Krishan Ji was only five years old when he succeeded his father and he is sometimes called the 'Child Guru'. He died of smallpox at the age of eight and named his great uncle as his successor. Many people who had smallpox were healed when they drank spring water which he gave to them.

There is a famous gurdwara called Bangla Sahib at the site of Guru Har Krishan Ji's place of death in Delhi.

Guru Tegh Bahadur Ji (1664–75)

Guru Tegh Bahadur Ji was the youngest son of Guru Har Gobind Ji. His name means 'brave sword'.

Many people plotted against Guru Tegh Bahadur Ji. He fought against the Mogul rulers who were destroying Sikh temples and forcing people to convert to Islam. The emperor had made Sikhs and Hindus pay large taxes, and closed their schools and temples. Guru Tegh Bahadur Ji fought the emperor and was arrested.

Four of the Guru's companions were executed while he was made to watch. Then he was also killed.

Guru Tegh Bahadur Ji is respected as he died protecting the liberty of Sikhs and Hindus. A gurdwara called Sis Ganj Sahib stands in Delhi where he was executed.

Peace and strife

Guru Har Gobind Ji established a court at the Akal Takht in Amritsar. He was imprisoned by the Mogul rulers, and had to spend the end of his life in Hindur, beyond the reach of the emperor.

Guru Har Rai Ji spent his time in prayer. He helped Dara Shikoh, who was leading a revolt against his brother Aurangzeb, the Mogul emperor. He said that, as a true Sikh, he had simply helped a man who needed help. When the Guru sent his son to the Mogul court, Ram Rai performed miracles, and altered a line of the Adi Granth to please the emperor.

When Guru Har Rai Ji chose Guru Har Krishan Ji as the next Guru, Ram Rai asked the Mogul emperor for help. The boy was called to Delhi during a severe cholera epidemic. Although he cured many people, he died of smallpox.

Guru Tegh Bahadur Ji was a very successful preacher, and converted many people to Sikhism. He was executed by the Moguls.

Guru Gobind Singh Ji

In this section you will:
- learn about the life of Guru Gobind Singh Ji
- learn about the teachings of Guru Gobind Singh Ji
- read about events at Baisakhi.

Guru Gobind Singh Ji (1666–1708)

Guru Gobind Singh Ji was nine years old when his father, Guru Tegh Bahadur Ji, was executed. He was the last human Guru, and probably the most famous after **Guru Nanak Dev Ji**.

Guru Gobind Rai Ji, as he was originally known, was very clever at languages and a skilled horseman, archer and hunter. He was also a great poet, and a book of his poems called the **Dasam Granth** (the Tenth Collection) is second in importance to the **Guru Granth Sahib Ji** itself.

Guru Gobind Rai Ji is remembered for two very important contributions to **Sikhism**.

He formed the **Khalsa**, the 'community of the pure', and he chose the **Adi Granth**, now called the Guru Granth Sahib Ji, to succeed him and to be the final Guru.

In 1699 CE Sikhs from all over the Punjab were gathered at Anandpur Sahib, which is in a valley at the foot of the Himalayas. This was **Baisakhi**, the time of the Hindu festival of the wheat harvest which is celebrated on 13 April.

Guru Gobind Rai Ji gave a new meaning to Baisakhi for Sikhs.

He asked for five men to give their life for their faith. Each man went into a tent and the Guru then came out with blood on his sword. After the fifth man had gone inside, the tent was opened to show that all five were alive and well.

These men, the **panj piare** ('Five Beloved Ones') had been prepared to die for their faith. This event was the founding of the Khalsa – the community of the pure. From now on, all Sikhs were encouraged to wear the **panj kakke** – five Ks. Guru Gobind Rai Ji also said that all Sikh males should take the name **Singh** meaning 'lion'; and Sikh females should take the name **Kaur** which means 'princess'. He then changed his name to Guru Gobind Singh Ji. He dissolved sugar crystals in water and

Guru Gobind Singh Ji with his sons

The Guru Granth Sahib Ji is the final Sikh Guru

stirred it with a **khanda** (a double-edged sword), then he sprinkled it over the panj piare.

The events at Baisakhi in 1699 CE marked the founding of the Khalsa and, since then, the festival of Baisakhi has been the beginning of the Sikh New Year.

Guru Gobind Singh Ji and his followers in Anandpur were under attack from the Mogul armies, and he and his wife had to leave. Many battles were fought between the Khalsa and the Moguls. During these battles, Guru Gobind Singh Ji lost his four sons and his mother. Countless numbers of Sikhs were killed, but more and more joined the ranks of the Khalsa.

Guru Gobind Singh Ji died of stab wounds in 1708 CE.

When he was dying, he took five coins and a coconut. He placed them in front of the Adi Granth. This was the way in which a new Guru was named, and so, by doing this, he was naming the Adi Granth as his successor. From then on, the Adi Granth was known as the Guru Granth Sahib Ji.

Soldier and poet

Guru Gobind Singh Ji was a soldier. He spoke Persian, Arabic, Sanskrit and Punjabi. He improved Sikh law, and was the author of the Dasam Granth – the 'Tenth Volume'. He created a strong military base for the Sikhs of the Punjab.

He wrote poetry and music to urge his soldiers on, and created a love of the sword, which he called his 'sacrament of steel'.

All his solders were totally committed to fighting for the ideals of Sikhism, and to gain religious and political freedom for Sikhs so that they could again live in peace.

In a battle near Ambala, Guru Gobind Singh Ji lost all of his four sons and, later, his wife and mother. The Guru himself was killed by a Pashtun tribesman from the hills, in revenge for the death of his own father.

Sikh leaders

In this section you will:
- learn about leaders in Sikhism
- find out about the work of the granthi.

There are no priests in **Sikhism**, but there is a person who is responsible for leading the services.

Anyone who is a member of the **Khalsa** can read from the **Guru Granth Sahib Ji**, but it is usual for a **gurdwara** to have a person who is specially trained. This person is called a **granthi**, or 'reader', and can be a man or a woman.

The granthi also has to look after the Guru Granth Sahib Ji.

In some gurdwaras the granthi is employed full time and this is funded by the local community. In small villages in the Punjab, as elsewhere, most granthis are part time and have other jobs. In larger gurdwaras the granthis works for the gurdwara full time.

Even when there is a full-time granthi, other people may read from the Guru Granth Sahib Ji and may also lead the worship and the singing.

As well as being responsible for worship in the gurdwara, some granthis may visit the sick and needy and comfort those who are mourning a death. However, Sikhs believe that these duties also belong to the whole of the Sikh community.

A granthi reading from the Guru Granth Sahib Ji

Ragis perform an important role in the gurdwara

As well as the granthi, a **ragi** is another important person in the gurdwara. During services a ragi sits to the side of the Guru Granth Sahib Ji and provides music for singing. The most common instruments are the baja, like a harmonium, and a tabla or jorri, which is a type of drum.

Granthis

There are no priests in Sikhism, and any member of the Khalsa can read from the Guru Granth Sahib Ji. People who are trained to do this are called granthi. Anyone, male or female, can become a granthi and can take on the responsibility of leading worship. In some religions such as Christianity, the religious leaders are priests, and they can perform special services and rites.

A granthi's duties

It is the responsibility of the granthi to look after the Guru Granth Sahib Ji, the Sikh scriptures. They see that it is laid to rest each night, and brought from its rest room to the prayer hall each morning.

Sikh beliefs about God

In this section you will:
- learn what Sikhs believe about God
- read about the importance of God's name to Sikhs.

The Mool Mantar

One of the central statements of Sikh belief is in a hymn called the **Mool Mantar**.

Mool Mantar means 'basic teaching' and it is found at the beginning of the **Guru Granth Sahib Ji**.

It is repeated each day during early morning prayer.

The first words of the Mool Mantar are **Ik Onkar** meaning 'There is one God'.

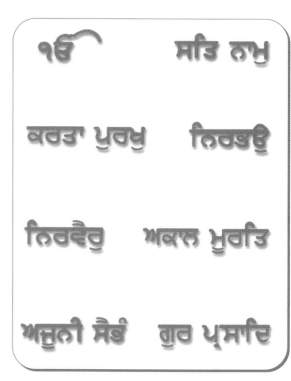

The Mool Mantar

The Mool Mantar	
Ik Onkar	There is only one God
Sat Nam	Eternal truth is God's name
Karta Purakh	God is the creator
Nir Bhau	God is without fear
Nir Vair	God is without hate
Akal Murat	Immortal, without form
Ajuni	Beyond birth and death
Saibhang	God is the enlightener
Gur Parshad	God can be reached through the mercy and grace of the true **Guru**

The symbol for Ik Onkar is seen in many places, such as badges, on the walls of a **gurdwara** and in the home. It is a constant reminder to Sikhs of their faith and belief in **Waheguru**.

Beliefs about God

The most important belief in **Sikhism** is that there is only one God – Waheguru. God is beyond the understanding of human beings. God cannot be described because humans can only describe God in human terms which will always be less than what God is. God is neither male nor female. God is the creator who created the world for people to use and enjoy. God is everywhere and beyond everything. God created people, and taught them the difference between right and wrong.

Although people know the difference between what is right and what is wrong, they still have to choose for themselves which path they will follow. God is present in everyone's soul, but can only be seen by those who are blessed. God is personal and is available to everyone.

Sikhs believe that the one God is the God of all religions. No one religion can claim to be the only true way to God and different religions are just different ways towards God. Therefore it is not important which God people worship. What is important is that they follow the teachings of God so that they have the chance of achieving **mukti**, or escape from rebirth.

You are Father, Mother, Friend, Brother, with you as support everywhere, what fear can I have?

Guru Granth Sahib Ji

> There are many names for God, such as:
>
> | | |
> |---|---|
> | Sat Nam | Eternal Reality |
> | Akal Purakh | Eternal One |
> | Waheguru | Wonderful Lord |

Nammarga

Sikhism is sometimes called nammarga – 'the way of nam' – because one of the important parts of Sikh worship it to repeat 'Japna', the name of God. Sikhs believe that repeating God's name helps to free them from any sin they have done. Once they have reached this stage, they can then work to overcome anger, attachment, greed, lust and pride. Nam Japna – saying Waheguru – 'Wonderful Lord' – helps Sikhs to concentrate – divya dristi. In this way, they can begin to open the dasam duar – the 'tenth gate' – which leads to mukti and escape from rebirth, so that they can rejoin God.

Unlike some other religions, Sikhism teaches that there is only one God, and Sikhs state this – Ik Onkar – each time they say the opening line of the Mool Mantar.

One very important Sikh belief is that Sikhs should keep the name of God in their minds and live their lives as God would wish.

Ik Onkar – the first words of the Mool Mantar

Sikh beliefs about life

In this section you will:
- learn what Sikhs believe about how they should live their lives
- find out about mukti.

Sikhs believe that everything that happens is **Hukam** – the will of God.

There is a part of God in each person and this soul is taken back to God when a person is finally released from the cycle of rebirth.

Sikhs believe that there are nearly eight and a half million different forms of life and that many souls have to be reborn through a large number of these before they can finally reach God. Each time something dies the soul is reborn. It is only humans who can know the difference between right and wrong and so it is only when the soul is in a human being that the cycle can be broken.

Karma – actions and their consequences – decide whether a soul can be set loose from the cycle. Freedom from this cycle is called **mukti**.

There are several things that can stop a soul reaching mukti:
- **a hankar** – pride
- **kam** – lust or desire
- **karodh** – anger
- **lobh** – greed
- **moh** – being too attached to the world

Prayer is an important part of Sikh worship

Sikhs believe in hard work and helping others

- **Manmukh** – being self-centred instead of God-centred (**gurmukh**)

- **Maya** – delusion, that is looking at the world and ignoring God.

Those who live without these devote their life to **sewa** – selfless service to others.

In order to avoid these dangers Sikhs are encouraged to follow these rules of conduct:

- There is only one God. Worship and pray to God alone, and remember God at all times.

- Always work hard, and share with others.

- Live a truthful life.

- Remember that men and women are equal in God's eyes.

- The whole human race is one. All distinctions are wrong.

- Idols, magic, omens, fasts, marks on the face and sacred threads are banned.

- Dress simply and modestly.

- **Khalsa** Sikh women should not wear the veil. Neither women nor men should make holes in their ears or noses.

- Live a married life.

- Put your faith in the **Guru Granth Sahib Ji.**

- Avoid lust, anger, greed, attachment to worldly things and arrogance.

- Live a humble and simple life.

Reincarnation

Reincarnation is the belief that a soul may be reborn many times into different forms of life. The form of life into which the soul is reborn will depend on the behaviour of the soul in its previous life. **Sikhism** teaches that it is only by being born as a human being that the soul has a real chance of being finally free to join God – **Waheguru** – because only humans have the ability to know the difference between right and wrong, and so to choose the correct way of life.

To reach mukti, or freedom, is the aim of all Sikhs. This is not because they do not enjoy their lives, but because they want to be released from the cycle of rebirth, so that the divine spark which is in all life can join God.

Signs and symbols 1

In this section you will:

● begin to learn what the five Ks mean, and how they are symbolized

● consider how wearing the five Ks affects Sikhs' lives.

Symbols are a way in which we remind ourselves, and other people, of important ideas and beliefs. Signs and symbols are used in everyday life and many religions have particular symbols of their own. Sikhism has many important symbols.

The five Ks

Sikhs who are members of the **Khalsa** (the community of the pure) have to wear five symbols; **kara**, **kangha**, **kesh**, **kachera** and **kirpan**. These **five Ks – panj kakke** – show that the person is a Sikh. They also have spiritual meanings and are symbols of the faith. They come from the establishment of the Khalsa by **Guru** Gobind Singh Ji at **Baisakhi** in 1699 CE and remind Sikhs of their beliefs and their history.

Kara

The **kara** is a bracelet, made of iron or steel, and worn on the right wrist. Some Sikhs wear two karas. The metal represents strength, and the circle is a symbol of unity and eternity which has no beginning and no end. This shows the Sikh view of God who is eternal and infinite. The circle also stands for the unity between Sikhs and between Sikhs and God.

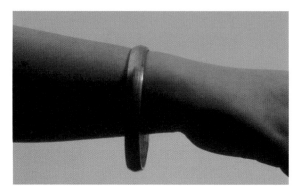
Kara

Kangha

The **kangha** is a comb used by Sikhs to keep their hair clean and tidy. Guru Gobind Singh Ji said that cleanliness was very important. Sikhs are encouraged to wash their hair early each morning. They then comb it and wind it into a topknot. The kangha is placed in the topknot to keep it in place. Sometimes the kangha has a small image of a **kirpan** (sword) on it. Using the khanga to keep their hair in place also reminds Sikhs of the need for discipline in order to live according to God's will.

Kangha

Kesh

Kesh

Kesh is uncut hair. Khalsa Sikhs do not cut their hair. Guru Gobind Singh Ji said that hair should be allowed to grow as God intended it to. Many Sikh men keep their hair covered with a **turban**, but this is not one of the five Ks. Some women also wear a turban. Young boys may wear a cloth over their topknot to keep their hair clean.

The five Ks

Signs and symbols are an important part of most religions, and also of life itself. Signs and symbols are also useful because they can often reach across languages and cultures.

The five Ks act as a constant reminder to Sikhs of who they are and what they believe in. They are first mentioned in the Rahatnamal, written by a follower of Guru Gobind Singh Ji.

Discrimination

Sometimes, Sikhs have suffered discrimination because of wearing some of the five Ks. The most problematic one is kesh – uncut hair. Any Khalsa Sikh who cuts their hair is a patit, or renegade. Many Sikhs wear turbans, which are traditional in the Punjab, and which help to keep the hair clean and tidy. It is often wearing turbans that has caused Sikhs to be the victims of racism.

Signs and symbols 2

In this section you will:

- learn about the kachera and the kirpan, and other Sikh symbols
- think about the importance of these symbols
- read about the symbolism of the Nishan Sahib.

Kachera

Kachera are short trousers that are usually worn as undergarments. They are worn by both men and women. **Guru** Gobind

Singh Ji said that Sikhs should wear these short trousers as part of the **Khalsa** uniform. Hindus usually wore dhotis (a long loin cloth) or long cloaks. Both of these garments were unsuitable for fighting in and the kachera may have made it easier for Sikhs to fight in a battle if they had to.

Wearing these clothes reminds Sikhs that they must always be prepared to defend their religion and the rights of other people to practise their own faith. Today, these short trousers are seen as a symbol of modesty for many Sikhs and remind them of the need to live a good life according to the teachings of the Gurus.

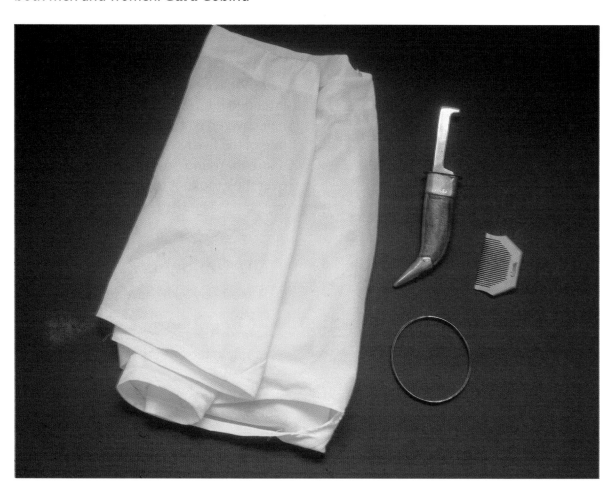

Kachera, kangha, kara and kirpan

Kirpan

The **kirpan** is a sword worn by members of the Khalsa. The kirpan is a reminder of the courage of the first five Sikhs, the **panj piare**, who were willing to let Guru Gobind Singh Ji cut off their heads with a kirpan for the sake of their religion. So it is a symbol of bravery and of faith in God.

The kirpan is worn as a symbol of the Sikh being willing to defend his or her faith, or to defend the weak or oppressed.

Taking the kirpan out of its sheath would be considered disrespectful by some Sikhs. The kirpan is worn on a belt that goes across the shoulder under a coat. Because the kirpan is seen as a weapon, Sikhs outside of the Punjab have sometimes been told that they are not allowed to wear it in public. They have objected to the kirpan being called a dagger or a knife because it suggests that they are carrying it as a weapon. Sometimes the kirpan is worn as a very small symbol on the **kangha**.

Nishan Sahib

The Sikh flag and symbol is called the **Nishan Sahib**. This flag always flies outside a **gurdwara**. It is a triangle of saffron or orange cloth. On the flag is the **khanda**. The khanda itself has three important symbols on it. The first is a double-edged sword (itself known as a khanda), which is used to stir **amrit** in gurdwara services. The second is the **kara** (circular bangle) given to Sikhs as a symbol of their unity and oneness with God. The third is two kirpans. The two kirpans represent spiritual power and

worldly power and were first earned by Guru Har Gobind Ji.

The flag is treated with great respect and is renewed each year at the festival of **Baisakhi**.

Ik Onkar

The first words of the **Mool Mantar** are **Ik Onkar** meaning 'There is only one God'. The symbol for Ik Onkar is seen in many places, such as badges, on the walls of a gurdwara and in the home.

The Nishan Sahib

The Nishan Sahib flies outside of every gurdwara. It is a triangular flag, made of orange or saffron cloth. In the middle of the flag is the khanda. This shows some of the basic ideas of Sikhism. The double-edged sword is in the middle, and represents Divine Knowledge. The sharp edges of the sword separate truth from lies. The kara, or chakar, which surrounds the khanda stands for the perfection of the eternal God – **Waheguru**. Finally, the two curved kirpans represent Miri – temporal authority – and Piri – spiritual authority. These two swords were first introduced by Guru Hargobind Dev Ji, and show that Sikhs must be concerned with the practical needs of society as well as the spiritual life. At the top of the flagpole is a khanda or spear which is covered with the same cloth as the flag.

The gurdwara

In this section you will:
- learn about the gurdwara
- think about the importance of these buildings
- gain an understanding of the importance of the gurdwara.

Gurdwara means 'the doorway of the **Guru**'. It is a building in which the Sikh holy book, the **Guru Granth Sahib Ji**, is kept, and it is a place where Sikhs worship together. A gurdwara is also a community centre for Sikhs.

Outside a gurdwara there are usually symbols which show what it is. There will be a flagpole flying the **Nishan Sahib**, the Sikh flag. This is triangular, orange or saffron in colour and on it is a symbol known as the **khanda**. This consists of two curved **kirpans** (swords), a khanda (double-edged sword) and a **kara** (circular bangle).

Shoes must not be worn in the main prayer hall of a gurdwara. There are also sinks so that people can wash their hands before worship, and a box of head coverings as people must cover their heads as a sign of respect. Anyone is welcome in a gurdwara as long as they have no traces of alcohol or tobacco on them.

In the main prayer hall there is a large carpeted area. There are no seats or chairs because the **sadhsangat** (congregation) sit cross-legged on the floor. Feet must not point towards the Guru Granth Sahib Ji. Women and men sometimes sit on opposite sides of the gurdwara so they do not distract each other during worship.

Sikhs in a gurdwara – the central place of Sikh community worship

The Guru Granth Sahib Ji being laid to rest for the night

At one end of the hall is the **manji** or sahib (a raised platform) with a **chanani** (canopy). There are cushions on the manji with **romalla** (beautiful cloths) draped over them. The romalla covers the Guru Granth Sahib Ji when it is not being read. The **granthi**, who may be a man or a woman, sits behind the Guru Granth Sahib Ji, facing the worshippers.

In front of the manji there is a long box called a **golak**, in which worshippers place their money offerings.

On another platform, the **ragis** (musicians) sit to play their instruments during **kirtan** (hymn singing). Music is an important aspect of Sikh worship. Verses from the scriptures are set to music and called **shabads**. The singing of shabads is called kirtan. The hymns found in the Guru Granth Sahib Ji are known as **Gurbani** which means 'the words of the Guru'.

It is important for Sikhs to remember the words of the shabads. Before a hymn is sung the ragis will read it and say a few words of explanation.

Inside a gurdwara there is a room which is the rest room for the holy scriptures. The rest room has a bed, with pillows, covers and a canopy. The Guru Granth Sahib Ji is 'put to bed' each night by the granthi or another Sikh who says the prayer, **Kirtan Sohila**. Each morning it is 'woken up' and placed on the manji.

Sikh places of worship

The first Sikh place of worship was built at Kartapur by **Guru Nanak Dev Ji**, and was called dharamsala – a place of faith.

A gurdwara is any building where there is a copy of Guru Granth Sahib Ji. The most important gurdwara is the Golden Temple in Amritsar, which was built by Guru Arjan Dev Ji to hold the first copy of the Guru Granth Sahib Ji. There are more than 200 historical gurdwaras, which have been built on particular sites associated with events in the life of one of the ten gurus. Many of these are centres for **yatras**, or pilgrimage, during Sikh festivals.

Around the world, Sikh communities build gurdwaras to provide a home for the Guru Granth Sahib Ji, and a centre for worship and community life. Some Sikhs set aside a room at home for a copy of the Guru Granth Sahib Ji, and so their houses become gurdwaras. Every gurdwara has a **langar**, where visitors are asked to share in a communal meal.

The langar

In this section you will:
- learn about the langar
- think about how the sharing of food might affect people lives
- consider the importance of sharing and equality in Sikhism.

Every **gurdwara** has a **langar** – 'Guru's kitchen' or eating area. The meal eaten here is also called a langar. The langar is part of worship and a very important aspect of Sikh life. There is no charge for the food served in the langar.

Guru Nanak Dev Ji set up the langar because he rejected the Hindu **caste** system where people of different castes are not allowed to eat together. Guru Nanak Dev Ji wanted to stress the idea that everyone is equal, so he wanted everyone to be able to eat the same food in the langar. Also, everyone was to share the tasks of preparation, cooking, serving and cleaning. This shows **sewa** – selfless service to others in the **sadhsangat** (community), to the gurdwara and to the world outside, and is a very important aspect of **Sikhism**.

This teaching was continued by Guru Amar Das Ji. He made a rule that no one could see him until they had first eaten in the langar.

Sikh families consider it a privilege to provide for the langar and to serve others. There is usually a waiting list of people who want to provide the langar each week.

Members of the sadhsangat (congregation) are served their food and sit in rows, on the

Sharing food together in the langar illustrates the equality of all people before God

Vegetarian food is served in the langar so as not to exclude anyone

floor or at long tables with benches. Food is usually served by the male members of the congregation. There are no special places and everyone eats the same food.

Although not all Sikhs are vegetarian, no meat is served in the langar so that no one will be excluded from the meal. Sikhs are not allowed to eat any meat which has been ritually slaughtered.

Communal eating

The first Sikh eating room was set up by Guru Nanak Dev Ji and Mardana in Sultanpur. This idea of a place in a gurdwara were everyone could eat together, regardless of race, religion or caste, was continued by the second and third gurus. Guru Amar Das Ji would not see anyone who had not first eaten in the langar. Even the Mogul emperor ate there before visiting the Guru.

Food and drink

Hindus do not eat beef, and many are vegetarians. Muslims and Jews do not eat pork. So, although Sikhs are not required to be vegetarian, no meat is served in the langar.

In the langar, the food is prepared by volunteers and is available at all times. On special occasions, the tea that is served in the langar may be made with milk which has been flavoured with spices, such as cinnamon.

Worship 1

There is no special day for Sikhs to worship, although Sunday is popular because it is a day when most people do not go to work. Some communities have their services daily or in the evenings.

Prayers are said every morning and evening in the **gurdwara**, but not all members of the local community attend these.

Congregational worship is called **diwan** or **kirtan**, which means hymn singing, because verses from the **Guru Granth Sahib Ji** are sung as part of the service.

The weekly service

After bathing, members of the **sadhsangat** (congregation) remove their shoes, cover their heads and wash their hands before entering the prayer hall.

Sikhs approach the **manji** or **sahib** (platform) on which the Guru Granth Sahib Ji is placed. They kneel on their hands and knees and lower their heads until their foreheads touch the floor as a sign of respect.

Then they make an offering of money, flowers or food for the use of the Sikh community.

Sikhs may then greet other members of the congregation by saying **Waheguru** before sitting cross-legged on the floor facing the manji. Men and women usually sit on opposite sides of the prayer hall.

The service may last for two hours or more.

Sikhs kneeling in front of the Guru Granth Sahib Ji

The Ardas is an important Sikh prayer

It begins early in the morning when the Guru Granth Sahib Ji is removed from its resting place and placed on the manji. There are readings from the Guru Granth Sahib Ji until the **ragis** (musicians) arrive. The readings are chosen at random.

People chant verses from the Guru Granth Sahib Ji and the ragis sing and accompany them on musical instruments. The congregation joins in the hymns. This part of the service is called kirtan.

A sermon is given by a member of the Sikh community. This is usually an explanation of the readings from the Guru Granth Sahib Ji.

At the end of the service, there are prayers which include six verses from **Anand Sahib**, a hymn written by Guru Amar Das Ji, the last part of the **Japji Sahib**, written by **Guru Nanak Dev Ji**, a verse from a hymn by Guru Arjan Dev Ji, and, finally, **Ardas**.

The congregation face the Guru Granth Sahib Ji with their hands together.

The first part of Ardas mentions God and all the Gurus. The second part reminds Sikhs that the Guru Granth Sahib Ji is God's word, and of the faithful Sikhs of the past. The final part of Ardas is a prayer asking God to keep the **Khalsa** faithful and for the well-being of people of all races and religions.

While Ardas is being said the **karah parshad** (a sweet food that is shared by the congregation) is prepared, by stirring it with a **kirpan**. After Ardas, everyone sits down. The karah parshad is offered first to five practising Sikhs, in memory of the **panj piare**, and then handed out to everyone present. This shared food shows that everyone is equal before God.

In the gurdwara

When a person goes into a gurdwara, they are expected to remove their shoes and to cover their head as a sign of respect to the Guru Granth Sahib Ji. People wash their hands and, sometimes, their feet as well. As people approach the Guru Granth Sahib Ji, they bow down and touch the floor.

Everyone sits on the floor so that the Guru Granth Sahib Ji is higher than everyone else. Although men and women sit separately, they sit at the same distance from the Guru Granth Sahib Ji.

People can enter or leave the gurdwara at any time during the service, but everyone is expected to stand facing the Guru Granth Sahib Ji when the Ardas is read. The distribution of karah parshad to everyone at the end of the service again stresses the essential Sikh teaching about equality.

Worship 2

In this section you will:

- learn about Sikh daily worship and its importance

- read about the continuous reading of the Guru Granth Sahib Ji, called the Akhand Path.

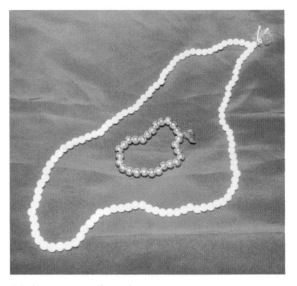

Mala – prayer beads

Nam Simran

Guru Nanak Dev Ji taught that the most important form of worship is **bhakti** (devotion to God). Some people say that the whole of **Sikhism** is bhakti.

When Sikhs meditate on, or think about, the name of God this is known as **Nam Simran** (thinking of the name). People sense God and grow ever closer to God.

Sikhs remember the presence of God through **Nam Japna**, repeating the name of God, **Waheguru**. This can be said aloud or silently.

Morning prayer

After bathing, meditate upon the Lord and your body and mind will become pure.

Guru Granth Sahib Ji

Guru Ram Das Ji said:

He who calls himself a Sikh of the great Sat Guru should rise early and meditate on God's name.

Guru Granth Sahib Ji

Sikhs get up early each day to pray and meditate. This is called **amritvela**. The early morning is peaceful and a good time for prayer and meditation. First, they take a bath, and get dressed. Then, after covering their heads, they can begin prayer.

Prayer begins with the **Japji Sahib**, a hymn of 38 verses which comes from the first section of the **Guru Granth Sahib Ji**. The opening verses of the Japji Sahib are the **Mool Mantar**. After the Japji Sahib, other prayers are said and some Sikhs will read hymns from a collection called the Gutka. At the end of prayers, Sikhs meditate. Some people use **mala** (prayer beads) to help them.

Prayers must not be said while doing other things and, ideally, should be done in a quiet place where there are no distractions.

Throughout the day, some Sikhs will often practise Nam Japna this is done by repeating the word 'Waheguru' under their breath.

Sikh women praying at home

Evening prayer

In the evening there are set hymns and prayers. **Sodar Rahiras** is said before the evening meal. Just before going to bed Sikhs will recite a small group of hymns called the **Kirtan Sohila**.

The Akhand Path

The **Akhand Path** is a continuous reading of the Guru Granth Sahib Ji. It takes place on special occasions, such as a marriage, and also during **gurpurbs**.

The Akhand Path takes eighteen hours, and the reading can be done by family members or by a **granthi**. After the reading is over, the Bhog ceremony takes place. The Guru Granth Sahib Ji is opened at random, and the hymn on the page is read.

History of the Akhand Path

The Akhand Path ceremony began in the eighteenth century, when there were very few copies of Guru Granth Sahib Ji available. Many Sikhs were fighting for their religion and their lives at this time, and were in hiding. Whenever they could, they would gather together to hear a reading from the Guru Granth Sahib Ji, before the book was moved.

The Guru Granth Sahib Ji

The **Guru Granth Sahib Ji** is the holy scripture of the Sikhs. The book is written in Punjabi using the **Gurmukhi** – 'from the mouth of the **Guru**' – script. Every copy of the Guru Granth Sahib Ji is exactly the same, with 1430 pages. The Guru Granth Sahib Ji can be translated, but these translations are not used in Sikh worship.

The Guru Granth Sahib Ji is a collection of the teachings and hymns of **Guru Nanak Dev Ji** and five of the other Sikh Gurus. It is treated as a living Guru by Sikhs, as Guru Gobind Singh Ji taught.

The second Guru, Guru Angad Dev Ji, wrote down the hymns of Guru Nanak Dev Ji. The third Guru, Guru Amar Das Ji, composed more hymns, including the **Anand Sahib** (Hymn of Bliss). The fourth Guru, Guru Ram Das Ji, composed the **Lavan**, the four verses which are sung at a wedding ceremony. The fourth Guru, Guru Arjan Dev Ji, brought all the hymns of the other Gurus into one single set of scriptures, known as the **Adi Granth**.

The Guru Granth Sahib Ji has 1430 pages of scripture

A page of the Guru Granth Sahib Ji written in Gurmukhi script

Guru Gobind Singh Ji added more hymns written by his father, Guru Tegh Bahadur Ji. He announced that, after his death, there would be no other living Guru, but that the scriptures should now become the Guru.

The Adi Granth then became a 'Guru' and was known as the Guru Granth Sahib Ji.

The Guru Granth Sahib Ji is given the same respect that was shown to the human Gurus during their lifetimes. It has a special resting place where it is put to bed every evening.

At the beginning of each day, the **granthi**, and any other Sikhs present, form a procession to carry the Guru Granth Sahib Ji to its position in the main prayer hall of the **gurdwara**.

The Guru Granth Sahib Ji is never placed on the ground and Sikhs never turn their back on it.

While the Guru Granth Sahib Ji is being read, the granthi waves a special fan, called a **chauri**, over the pages of the book. This chauri has a long handle and is made from yak hair. It remembers the **pakha,** which was used by Sikhs walking with the Gurus to keep them cool in the hot areas of the Punjab.

The Guru Granth Sahib Ji is of very great importance for Sikhs, who believe that it is **Gurbani** or the word of God.

Many Sikhs own a copy of the Guru Granth Sahib Ji and take care to show it respect.

Some Sikh families have a copy of the **Dasam Granth** (poetry written by Guru Gobind Singh Ji and not included in the Guru Granth Sahib Ji) or the sacred **Nit nem** (a prayer book) at home.

The word of God

The Guru Granth Sahib Ji is different from the holy books of other religions because, as well as the writings of six of the Gurus, it contains works by people from other faiths. Sikhs do not worship idols, and so the respect they show for the Guru Granth Sahib Ji is for the writings which it contains, which are Gurbani – the word of God.

Most of the writings are in Punjabi, but there are also hymns in Persian, medieval Hindi, Sanskrit and Arabic. Each of the 1430 pages has eighteen or nineteen lines of Gurmukhi – 'from the mouth of the Guru' – script which was developed by Guru Angad Dev Ji.

The hymns are arranged according to the tune to which they are sung, then by the type of poem and, finally, by the key in which they are sung.

Festivals 1

In this section you will:

- learn about Sikh festivals and how these are celebrated
- read about the main gurpurbs celebrated in Sikhism.

There are two different types of festivals in **Sikhism**:

- Special holy days which celebrate events in the lives of the **Gurus**. These are known as **gurpurbs** – Gurus' remembrance days.
- Other celebrations are held on the same days as some Hindu festivals. These are known as **melas**.

Gurpurbs

The gurpurbs are days that remember the births and deaths of the Gurus. Some of these are particularly important. They include:

- the martyrdom of Guru Arjan Dev Ji (May/June) (16 June)
- the installation of the **Guru Granth Sahib Ji** (August/early September)
- the birthday of **Guru Nanak Dev Ji** (November)
- the birthday of Guru Gobind Singh Ji (December) (5 January)
- the martyrdom of Guru Tegh Bahadur Ji (December) (24 November).

Part of the celebration of a gurpurb is a complete reading of the Guru Granth Sahib Ji. This is called the **Akhand Path**.

The Guru Granth Sahib Ji being carried through the streets at a gurpurb

Sikhs celebrating the birthday of Guru Nanak Dev Ji

Sikhs usually come to the **gurdwara** on the last day to hear the last pages of the Guru Granth Sahib Ji being read.

In India, these events are celebrated on the actual day, but in other countries, they are usually celebrated on the closest Sunday. The Akhand Path begins on Friday and ends at the Sunday service.

In India, the Guru Granth Sahib Ji is traditionally carried through the streets in a procession with five men representing the **panj piare**.

Gurpurbs

Gurpurbs are important anniversaries associated with the lives of the Gurus. There is usually a reading of the Akhand Path, which ends on the actual day when the gurpurb is celebrated. There is also **kirtan** (hymn singing from from the Guru Granth Sahib Ji) and katha (lectures on Sikhism). In some gurdwaras, there is nagar kirtan, when the Guru Granth Sahib Ji is carried in procession by five Sikhs.

Main gurpurbs

● The first installation of the Guru Granth Sahib Ji in the Golden Temple by Guru Arjan Dev Ji in August 1604 CE.

● The birth of Guru Nanak Dev Ji on 15 Apri 1469 CE in the Western Punjab village of Talwandi.

● The birth of Guru Gobind Singh Ji on 22 December 1666 CE at Patna.

● The martyrdom of Guru Arjan Dev Ji on 30 May 1606 CE in the River Ravi.

Festivals 2

In this section you will:
- learn more about how Sikh festivals are celebrated
- read about the festivals of Sangrand and Maghi.

Changing the Nishan Sahib at Baisakhi

Mela

There are three major Sikh festivals which are held on the same day as Hindu festivals. They are:

- **Baisakhi**
- **Divali Mela**
- **Hola Mohalla Mela**.

The word **mela** means a fair.

Guru Amar Das Ji said that Sikhs should come together for worship during Baisakhi and Divali Mela, and Guru Gobind Singh Ji added Hola Mohalla Mela. Celebrating these festivals showed that Sikhs were a separate religious group and that they no longer celebrated the festivals as Hindus do.

Baisakhi

Baisakhi is the month of the wheat harvest in the Punjab. The festival is on 13 April and marks the Sikh New Year.

In 1699 CE Guru Gobind Singh Ji founded the **Khalsa** at Baisakhi. Sikhs also remember 1919 CE when 400 Sikhs (many of them women and children) were killed by British soldiers who had been ordered to stop their Baisakhi celebrations at Jallianwala Bagh in **Amritsar**.

The **Nishan Sahib** (Sikh flag) is changed at Baisakhi. During the festival, the **Akhand Path** is read and initiation ceremonies (**Amrit**) are held.

Divali Mela

Divali Mela is celebrated throughout India in the autumn, and marks the end of the rainy season.

Sikhs remember the story of Guru Har Gobind Ji who returned to Amritsar on Divali. He had been in prison while the Mogul emperor, Jehangir, tried to stop the growth of **Sikhism**. The emperor was sick and his doctors said he could only be cured if he released the Guru. Guru Har Gobind Ji was released, but said that he would not go unless he could take 52 Hindu princes who were also in prison with him.

Jehangir told the Guru that he would free as many princes as could hold on to his clothes as he walked through a narrow passage. Guru Har Gobind Ji made himself a coat with long tassels, and all the princes went with him.

The Golden Temple during the festival of Divali Mela

Many Sikh homes are decorated with divas (clay lamps), candles and coloured lights. There are special meals and firework displays. It is a time of rejoicing. People give sweets to their friends and relatives. Services are held in **gurdwaras** and the Golden Temple in Amritsar is lit up.

Hola Mohalla Mela

In 1700 CE Guru Gobind Singh Ji held a three-day festival at **Anandpur Sahib**. This became a time for Sikhs to train as soldiers.

Hola Mohalla means 'attack and counter-attack'.

Sangrand

The festival of Sangrand is the start of each new month in the Indian calendar. In the gurdwaras, the Bara Maha, the 'Song of the Twelve Months', by Guru Arjan Dev Ji, is read and, sometimes, the Bara Maha, by Guru Nanak Dev Dev Ji, too. Sangrand is otherwise no more important than any other day.

Maghi

Maghi takes place on the first day of Maghar Sangrant, which is about 14 January. Sikhs go to gurdwaras to hear kirtan, in order to mark the martyrdom of the Forty Immortals. These were followers of Guru Gobind Singh Ji. They had been deserters, but they returned to help him to fight the Moguls, and were killed. They were blessed by the Guru, who said that they had achieved **mukti** by their bravery.

Pilgrimage 1

In this section you will:

● learn about some places that Sikhs might visit on pilgrimage

● gain an understanding of what Sikhs believe to be 'true pilgrimage'.

There are no special times for pilgrimage in **Sikhism**. Many Sikhs try to visit the places associated with their religion. Sikhs believe that God is everywhere, and so no one place is more holy than another.

The **Gurus** taught that it was not important to make special journeys to visit holy places.

True pilgrimage consists of the contemplation of the name of God and the cultivation of inner knowledge.

Guru Granth Sahib Ji

There is no place of pilgrimage equal to the Gurus. The Guru alone is the pool of contentment. The Guru is the river from which pure water is obtained, by which the dirt of evil understanding is washed away.

Guru Granth Sahib Ji

The Punjab in India is the homeland of Sikhs and more than half of the people who live there are Sikhs and speak Punjabi. Of the world population of more than 19 million Sikhs, 80 per cent live in the Punjab. Other Sikhs may also visit the Golden Temple at **Amritsar** and places

Harimandir Sahib – the Golden Temple – is a very important centre of pilgrimage for Sikhs

which are associated with the Gurus and their lives. These visits are called **yatras**.

The Harimandir Sahib

The most popular place to go on a yatra is the **Harimandir Sahib** – the Golden Temple at Amritsar. Harimandir means God's House.

The Harimandir Sahib is a very special **gurdwara**. The first Guru, **Guru Nanak Dev Ji**, chose the site and said that the fourth Guru would build there. Guru Ram Das Ji began to build a large pool there, which he filled with **amrit** (nectar), and named it Amritsar. This sort of pool is called a **serovar**. His son, Guru Arjan Dev Ji, built the Harimandir Sahib on an island in the middle of the serovar in 1601 CE.

The Harimandir Sahib has always been a major meeting place for Sikhs. The Mogul emperors destroyed the temple and filled in the serovar. In 1740 CE the temple was used as a hall for dancing and drinking. Two Sikhs travelled from the south of India to kill the ruler of Amritsar and to restore the temple.

The dome and the upper walls of the Harimandir Sahib are covered in gold leaf. There is a door on each of the four walls to show that the Harimandir Sahib is open to everyone. A long marble walkway crosses the serovar to the west door of the Harimandir Sahib, while a wide promenade called the Pakirama runs round the pool. There are also rows of rooms where pilgrims can rest. The **langar** in the Harimandir Sahib is open every day and anyone can eat there. The langar provides daily food for many of the poor people of Amritsar.

True pilgrimage

Sikhism teaches that a true pilgrimage is found in thinking about the name of God, and so reaching a better understanding of life. This is far more important than visiting special places. God is everywhere, so no place can be any more holy than any other.

Guru Nanak Dev Ji refused to take part in Hindu pilgrimages. In particular, he was opposed to people making pilgrimages to the Hindu sacred River Ganges. It was while Lehna, later to be Guru Angad Dev Ji, was on his way to the shrine of a Hindu goddess that he met Guru Nanak Dev Ji in 1532 CE. Guru Nanak Dev Ji refused to go with Lehna, and it was then that Lehna decided to become his follower.

The Golden Temple, at Amritsar in the Punjab, the most popular place for Sikhs to visit, has been attacked many times in its history. The most recent was on 6 June 1984, when Indian troops entered the temple during an armed struggle.

Pilgrimage 2

In this section you will:
- learn about why Sikhs may visit other places of pilgrimage
- read about four takhts in addition to the Akal Takht.

Akal Takht

Akal Takht means 'the Throne of the Eternal'. The Akal Takht faces the Golden Temple and was built by **Guru** Har Gobind Ji in 1609 CE. The building is used by Sikhs for political meetings and is the meeting place of the **Khalsa**. The highest Sikh court meets at the Akal Takht.

The Akal Takht houses the most sacred copy of the **Guru Granth Sahib Ji**. Each day, at 5 am in winter and 4 am in summer, it is carried in a golden carriage to the **Harimandir Sahib**. It is carried back to rest at 10 pm in winter and 11 pm in summer. Outside the building are two large flagpoles. One has the flag of Miri – temporal (earthly) authority, and the other of Piri – spiritual authority.

Anandpur Sahib

Anandpur Sahib is another special place for Sikhs. It is in a valley at the foot of the Himalayas. The ashes of the head of Guru Tegh Bahadur Ji are buried there and it is also the place where Guru Gobind Singh Ji founded the Khalsa. The most important celebrations for the festival of **Hola Mohalla Mela** take place at Anandpur.

Goindwal

Guru Amar Das Ji had a very deep well, or baoli, built at **Goindwal**. It provided safe drinking water and was surrounded by trees to improve the environment. It became a tradition for people to bathe in the well. People say the **Japji Sahib** on each of the 84 steps. Some people say that, by doing this, they will get nearer to **mukti**.

Pilgrimage, austerity [living simply], mercy, almsgiving and charity bring merit, be it as little as a mustard seed, but those who hear, believe and cherish the word, an inner pilgrimage and cleansing is theirs.

From the Japji Sahib

The Gurus said that ceremonial bathing served no purpose. When people recite the Japji Sahib going down into the well, they do not benefit from the bathing but because they have meditated on God's name.

If someone goes to bathe at a place of pilgrimage with the mind of a crook and the body of a thief then his outside will have been washed but his inside will be dirty twice over … The saints are good even without such washing. The thief remains a thief even if they bathe at a place of pilgrimage.

Guru Granth Sahib Ji

Other takhts

There are four other takhts in addition to the Akal Takht.

Takht Sri Damdama Sahib is in the village of Talwandi Sabo near Bhatinda. Guru Gobind Singh Ji stayed here for a year in 1705 CE, while he put together the final edition of the Guru Granth Sahib Ji.

Takht Sri Keshgarh Sahib is at Anandpur Sahib. The Khalsa was founded here by Guru Gobind Singh Ji in 1699 CE, and some of his weapons are kept here. The most important of these is the actual **khanda** used by Guru Gobind Singh Ji to prepare the **amrit** during the first Khalsa initiation ceremony.

Takht Sri Hazur Sahib is in Maharashtra, on the banks of Godavari, and is where Guru Gobind Singh Ji died in 1708 CE. The inner part of the temple stands over the site where he was cremated.

Takht Sri Patna Sahib is in Patna. It is the birthplace of Guru Gobind Singh Ji. The Guru was born here in 1666 CE, and spent his childhood here before moving to Anandpur.

The entrance to the well at Goindwal

Growing up

In this section you will:

- learn about Sikh birth and initiation ceremonies
- gain an understanding of the ethical code followed by Khalsa Sikhs.

Birth

As soon as a baby is born, many Sikhs whisper the words of the **Mool Mantar** in its ear and place a drop of honey on its tongue.

The name-giving ceremony

Once the mother and child are well enough to go out, there is a special ceremony held at the **gurdwara**.

The **granthi** opens the **Guru Granth Sahib Ji** at random. The baby's name will begin with the first letter of the first hymn on the left-hand side of the page. The parents are then given some time to choose a name. This name is announced by the granthi who adds the title **Singh** for a boy or **Kaur** for a girl. The granthi then shouts 'Jo bole so nihal' (Whoever believes in the Truth will be saved) and the congregation reply 'Sat sri akahl' (The Truth is eternal).

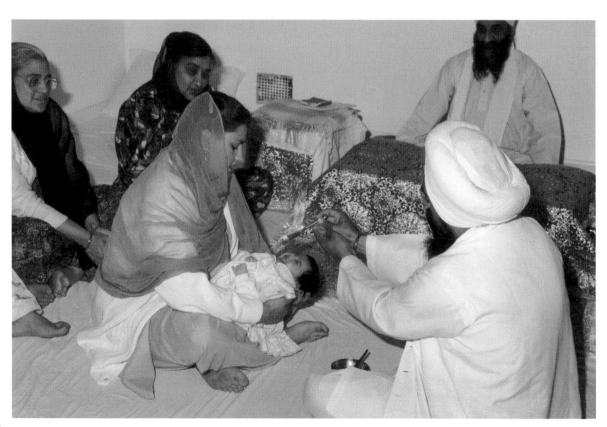

The name-giving ceremony is a special occasion, which takes place in the gurdwara

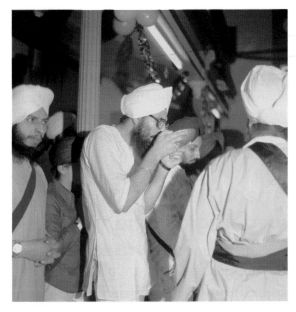

The Amrit ceremony is the initiation ceremony for Khalsa Sikhs

The ceremony ends with the **Anand Sahib** (Hymn of Bliss) and **karah parshad** is given to the congregation.

Initiation into the Khalsa

Boys and girls aged fourteen or sixteen are able to join the **Khalsa**. These Sikhs must have the **panj kakke** – the five Ks.

The ceremony is called **Amrit** and is conducted by five members of the Sikh community, representing the **panj piare**. They wear robes: tunics in orange or saffron, a blue sash around their waist and over the shoulder and a blue or orange turban.

One of the five Khalsa members explains the principles of the Sikh faith and reminds the candidates of the teachings of the Guru Granth Sahib Ji. The candidates for initiation are asked if they accept these. The five members of the Khalsa then kneel around an iron bowl, and prepare amrit from sugar and water. The liquid is stirred with a **khanda** (a double-edged sword).

Hymns are sung from the Guru Granth Sahib Ji and the candidates drink the amrit. These words are said: 'The Khalsa is of God, the victory is to God.' The amrit is sprinkled on the hair and eyes of the candidates five times, and then the Mool Mantar is read. **Ardas** is said and karah parshad distributed to everyone.

Sikhs who do not join the Khalsa are called **Sahaj-dhari** – 'seekers after God'.

An ethical code

Members of the Khalsa live according to an ethical code – Reht Maryada:

Sikhs will worship only God.

Sikhs must put their faith in the Guru Granth Sahib Ji.

Sikhs do not believe in fasts, sacred thread and traditional death rites.

The Khalsa must wear the five Ks.

The Khalsa pray to God before starting work.

Sikhs may learn other languages, but they must learn Punjabi.

Every male must add 'Singh' to his name and every female 'Kaur'.

Sikhs must not cut their hair.

Drugs, smoking and alcohol are forbidden.

Khalsa men and women must not have their ears or nose pierced.

Sikhs must live on honest labour and give to the poor.

Sikhs must not steal or gamble.

Marriage

In this section you will:

● learn about the Sikh marriage ceremony

● read and reflect upon some of the Sikh marriage customs.

Marriage is a very important part of **Sikhism**. Sometimes two families may bring a couple together, but the couple both have the right not to marry. Sikhs believe it is important that the families can get on with each other. This is why Sikhs do not encourage people to marry outside of their religion.

There is sometimes an engagement ceremony in the **gurdwara**, where God is thanked for bringing the couple together. After this, the groom's mother visits the bride and gives her a gold ring to wear.

Anand karaj – the wedding ceremony

A Sikh wedding usually takes place in the morning. It is held in front of a copy of the **Guru Granth Sahib Ji**. In India a bride may be dressed in red, but elsewhere the bride may wear white and be dressed very simply. Her head will be covered with a chunni (scarf). The groom wears a coloured **turban** and scarf and carries a **kirpan**.

 A Sikh wedding in India

The Lavan ceremony in Britain

Before the service begins there is a ceremony called the **Milna**. The two families meet and give gifts and then eat a meal.

The ceremony begins with the morning hymn **Asa di var** and **Ardas**.

The first part explains that marriage is not just a social contract but the joining together of two souls.

The bride and groom bow to the Guru Granth Sahib Ji to show that they accept these teachings and want to spend the rest of their lives together.

The bride's father places flower garlands over the couple and then takes one end of the groom's scarf and ties it to the end of the bride's head scarf. This shows that she is leaving her father and joining her husband.

The **Lavan** (wedding hymn) of Guru Ram Das Ji is sung and after each of the four verses the couple walk clockwise around the Guru Granth Sahib Ji, the bride following the groom. Each time, they bow to the Guru Granth Sahib Ji.

The service ends with the sharing of **karah parshad**.

Everyone eats a meal in the **langar** after the ceremony.

Sikhs are expected to remain faithful to their husband or wife, and marriage is important to Sikhs because of strengthening family life and bringing up children. Sikhs accept that divorce is sometimes inevitable. Widows and widowers are allowed to remarry in a gurdwara.

Marriage customs

Sikhs must not choose their marriage partner on the basis of their **caste**.

A Sikh's daughter must be married to a Sikh.

Members of other religions cannot be married at the Anand Karaj ceremony.

No Sikh can accept a marriage partner for their son or daughter on the basis of money.

Sikhs must not consult horoscopes in order to choose the wedding date.

The congregation sits in front of the Guru Granth Sahib Ji. The bride sits on the groom's left, facing the Guru Granth Sahib Ji. The person conducting the service asks the man and woman to stand, and then offers the Ardas.

The person conducting the ceremony explains to the bride and groom the principles of Sikh marriage, and the idea of 'a single soul in two bodies'.

The groom is told that the bride has chosen him, and that he should look on her as his better half.

Death

In this section you will:
- learn the Sikh teachings about death
- gain an understanding of Sikh funeral customs.

For Sikhs, death is not the end. They believe in eternal life, or **reincarnation**. This means that a soul may be reborn many times as a human or an animal.

The **Guru Granth Sahib Ji** teaches that the body is clothing for the soul and so is not important, just as we might throw away old clothes.

Usually, Sikhs cremate their dead. In India this often happens on the day when someone dies, but elsewhere it may take place two or three days later, so that people have the chance to travel to the funeral.

When someone is dying their friends and relatives will come to their bedside and say **Sukhmani** (the Hymn of Peace).

A Sikh funeral ceremony – the body is placed in front of the Guru Granth Sahib Ji

The body is taken for cremation

The dying person will try to reply **Waheguru** (Wonderful Lord). The dead body is washed and dressed in traditional Sikh clothing, including the **five Ks** – **panj kakke**. It is placed in a coffin and taken to the **gurdwara**.

The coffin is carried to the cremation ground while hymns are sung. In India it is placed on a funeral pyre which is then lit by a close relative. As the coffin burns, someone says the evening prayer – the **Kirtan Sohila**:

All must receive their last call from the Master; daily he summons those souls who must go.

Hold in remembrance the Lord who will summon you; soon you will hear his command.

Kirtan Sohila

This shows the belief that death is just a short sleep before rebirth and that everyone must remember God in the hope of reaching **mukti**.

The relatives and friends of the dead person now return to the gurdwara where the **Anand Sahib** is sung, and **Ardas** is said. The ceremony ends with **karah parshad**.

Mourning

During the next ten days many families stay at home and are visited by friends and relatives. Karah parshad and **langar** are prepared by the family and offered to all visitors.

Some families arrange an **Akhand Path** (complete reading) or **Sadharan Path** (non-continuous reading) of the Guru Granth Sahib Ji after a funeral.

Funeral customs

Guru Nanak Dev Ji taught that funerals should not be carried out with any of the ceremonials associated with other religions. He said that the dead body should be shown respect, but that it was no longer of any value. The important part of the person, their soul, had already left the body to be reborn. **Guru Nanak Dev Ji** taught that there will be a Last Judgment and that, after this, souls which have been reincarnated will eventually rejoin Waheguru.

Mourners must not cry out at a funeral or make any public displays of their grief. Hymns are sung until the body is on the funeral pyre, and then a final prayer is said before the pyre is lit.

When the funeral pyre is burnt out, all the ashes are gathered up and either poured into running water or buried at the site of the cremation. Sikhs must not raise tombstones or monuments to the dead.

Creation

In this section you will:

● learn what Sikhs believe about creation

● read about Sikh beliefs about Waheguru, the Creator God.

Sikhism is based on the 'Oneness of Creation'. Sikhs believe that the universe was made by God who created the earth and all forms of life on it. God is in charge and arranges the birth, life and death of everything.

Humans, trees, holy places
Coasts, clouds, fields
Islands, continents, universes
Spheres and solar systems

Life forms – egg-born, womb-born, earth-born, sweat-born Only God knows their existence in oceans, mountains, everywhere Nanak says God created them and God takes care of them all.

Guru Granth Sahib Ji

Before the creation there was no earth, no sky, no sun and no life. Only God existed alone until God's decision to create the world. Then God created everything by a single word:

God spoke once and there was creation.

God is responsible for all of creation and everything in and on the earth belongs to God. God is in charge of all life and without God's **Hukam** (will) nothing can exist, change or develop.

God still looks after the world and protects it and Sikhism believes that all creatures lead their lives under God's rule.

If I were a doe living in the forest, eating grass and leaves, with God's Grace I will find God.
If I were a cuckoo living in the mango tree, contemplating and singing, God reveals through God's mercy.
If I were a female snake, dwelling in the ground, let God's word be in my being, my dread would vanish.
Eternal God is found, light meets light.

Guru Granth Sahib Ji

Sikhism teaches that God created five elements – air, water, earth, fire and space. Everything in nature is made from these elements. Water is the most important of the elements, but they must all be kept in balance to avoid disaster.

Waheguru, the Creator God

Sikhism teaches that it is God – Waheguru – who created everything and who is in charge of all life, arranging birth, life and death. Without God's will, nothing could exist. However, God is still actively involved in the world, caring for and protecting it and all life under God's will.

In the Guru Granth Sahib Ji, God is described as the creator.

'You are the Creator, O Lord, the Unknowable. You created the Universe of diverse kinds, colours and qualities. You know your own Creation. All this is your Play.'

Guru Nanak Dev Ji

Environment

In this section you will:

● learn how Sikhs care for the environment

● learn why this is important for Sikhs.

Sikhs believe that God created the world as a place where every type of plant and animal could live so that all life could have the chance to prove that it was good enough to reach **mukti**.

Guru Nanak Dev Ji taught that:

Nature we see
Nature we hear
Nature we observe with awe, wonder and joy
Nature in the nether regions
Nature in the skies
Nature in the whole creation
Nature in the sacred texts (Vedas, Puranas and Qur'an)
Nature in all reflection
Nature in food, in water, in garments and in love for all
Nature in species, kinds, colours
Nature in life forms
Nature in good deeds
Nature in pride and in ego
Nature in air, water and fire
Nature in the soil of the earth
All nature is yours, O powerful Creator
You command it, observe it and pervade within it.

Guru Granth Sahib Ji

Sikhs believe that humans are the stewards of the earth and have to look

Sikhs working to save the environment

Sikhs condemn oil pollution because it damages the environment

after it. They also believe that God's spirit is in everything, and therefore many Sikhs are vegetarians.

Sikhs believe that they must take care not to disturb the balance of nature. In the Punjab, rainfall is vital and always welcomed. When the monsoon arrives Sikhs celebrate because God has been good to them.

Sikhs are forbidden to kill for the sake of killing.

The Gurus have strongly made us aware of our responsibility towards this earth.

Guru Granth Sahib Ji

Sikhs believe that the environment can only be preserved if the balance God created is maintained. The principles for this are found in the Guru Granth Sahib Ji:

Pray to God – remember God and God's authority always;
Earn an honest living – do not take what does not belong to you, or more than you need – essential truths for a proper relationship with nature;
Share with others – this includes all creation, not just human beings.

Guru Granth Sahib Ji

Caring for life

Sikhism was founded in Punjab, in north-west India. The geographical situation of Punjab is such that rainfall is essential and, therefore, always welcomed. The arrival of rain is an occasion for rejoicing. Water is seen as a source of life. It produces vegetation which is used as food for humans and fodder for animals.

Sikhism teaches that the natural environment and the survival of all life forms are closely linked in the rhythm of nature. It is for this reason that, in Sikhism, those who kill for lust of hunting, eating or to make sacrifices are condemned.

In Sikh hymns, God is often referred to as the provider for all life, which God loves, and which loves God. God, as both father and mother, guarantees equality to man and woman in faith and compassion towards all beings and nature.

From the Sikh Statement on Nature made at Assisi, Italy, 1986

Human rights

It is a very important teaching of **Sikhism** that everyone is equal regardless of race, sex, class, **caste** or religion. Any hungry person who visits a **gurdwara** will always be fed.

Sikhs believe that God, who is the creator

A Hindu Brahmin during Divali. Guru Nanak Dev Ji taught that the caste system was wrong

and source of all forms of life, is without any form, gender or colour. Any differences between humans are unimportant – they do not make any one person better than any other. Any act of kindness which is performed towards another human being is seen as an act of worship to God.

Guru Nanak Dev Ji was born a Hindu, and Sikhism has kept some of the teachings of Hinduism. For example, Hinduism also welcomes people of all religious beliefs. However, Guru Nanak Dev Ji taught that the caste system of Hinduism was wrong.

There are four varnas (castes) which form divisions within Hindu society. Within these varnas, there are also many jati (caste groups). Hindus believe that every Hindu is born into a particular caste because of their behaviour in a previous life and that these cannot be changed.

The caste system affects almost everything a Hindu does. Marriages should only take place between members of the same caste. Some Hindus will not eat with, or take food from, members of castes lower than theirs.

Guru Nanak Dev Ji wanted the caste system to be abolished. Unfortunately some people still believe that it is important and it can sometimes influence aspects of Sikh life such as marriage, where members of one group may be unwilling to marry a member of another.

However, Sikhs are taught to treat all people equally and hope to be treated the same.

The langar is a place where Sikhs can offer hospitality to all

A Sikh independent homeland

One of the major problems for Sikhs today in seeking equality is Khalistan. In 1799 CE Maharaja Ranjit Singh established Lahore as the capital of an independent Sikh state where true equality among Sikhs, Muslims, Hindus and others was practised. The British took over the Punjab in 1849 CE and ended Sikh independence. When India became independent from Britain in 1947 CE, two countries were established: India was mainly Hindu and Pakistan was mainly Muslim. The Punjab was split between India and Pakistan. Sikhs asked for independence but it was not given to them. In 1966 CE the Indian government agreed that the province of the Punjab should have Punjabi as its official language and that Sikhs should represent the province in the Punjabi Suba (assembly). However, Sikhs are still working to reunite the Punjab into one country of their own.

The Punjab

The origins of the Punjab were in 1709–10, when a Sikh leader, Bandha Singh Bahadur, freed the land from Mogul rule. The Sikhs built the Punjab into a powerful kingdom under Ranjit Singh (1780–1839).

In 1849 CE, the Punjab came under British rule. The massacre of Jallianwala Bagh in 1919 brought 400 Sikh deaths and 1200 injuries. In 1947, when India gained its independence from Britain, the Punjab was split between India and Pakistan.

In 1966, the Punjab was divided into two. The new, smaller state of Punjab has its capital at Chandigarh.

By 1980, many Sikhs were campaigning for a totally independent Sikh homeland: Khalistan – Land of the Pure.

Service to others 1 – sewa

In this section you will:

● learn why the idea of sewa is so important to Sikhs

● read about different types of sewa in Sikhism.

It is very important for all Sikhs to provide a service to the community – **sewa**. This includes service to the Sikh community itself and others. Sikhs should give up some of their time and energy to help others. **Sikhism** comprises service to God, to the **Khalsa** and to all of humanity.

Tan – physical service: helping in the langar

Sikhism teaches that a person should try to become less self-centred (**manmukh**) and more God-centred (**gurmukh**) and so live their lives to help others (sewa).

Although **Nam Simran** (remembering God) is central to Sikhism, this must be combined with sewa. The following words from the **Guru Granth Sahib Ji** emphasize this point:

> True worship consists in the meditation of God's name … There can be no worship without performing good deeds.
>
> Guru Granth Sahib Ji

There are three different aspects of sewa:

● **Tan** – this is physical service and might include working in the **langar** and helping to look after the **gurdwara**. Providing langar for the congregation is seen as a privilege as well as a duty.

● **Man** – this is mental service. Sikhs might do this by studying the Guru Granth Sahib Ji and teaching it to others.

● **Dhan** – this is material service to other people. Sikhs might give money to charities or give their time to help people who are in need. It might also include building a school or a hospital, visiting the sick or caring for disaster victims.

All of these services should be performed because a Sikh wants to serve God. Therefore, Sikhs can perform sewa and so serve God and the world.

Tan – physical service: sweeping the pavements of the Golden Temple

The Gurus set the example of sewa by performing basic tasks which some people would have considered to be beneath them, for example cleaning the gurdwara.

A place in God's court can only be attained if we do service to others in this world … Wandering ascetics, warriors, celibates, holy men, none of them can obtain **mukti** without performing sewa.

Guru Granth Sahib Ji

Serving others

The Sikh Gurus said that sewa, the performance of selfless service to others, was the first step towards being a Sikh. A person who does service without payment or any hope of a reward is called a Sewak or Sewadar. Performing sewa makes people humble and, in this way, the name of God can enter into their mind.

A Sewak must have absolute faith in the Guru, and must follow the Sikh code of self-discipline.

Example of sewa

Physical service might be cleaning or looking after shoes at the gurdwara, or cooking in the langar. Sikhs might help the community or their family, and they might give money to the poor and to charities. Service with the mind may be thinking about the **Gurbani**, and remembering and repeating God's name. Anyone who performs sewa with an idea of gaining from it is not acting as a true Sikh.

Service to others 2

In this section you will:
- learn about Sikh principles of life
- consider how these principles affect Sikhs and why they are important.

The **Gurus** said that Sikhs should live their lives according to three principles which are all equally important:

- **Nam Simran** – to remember the name of God. This can be done by meditating on God's name.

- **Kirat karna** – to earn a living by honest means.

- **Vand chhakna** – to share everything in charity with people who are less fortunate.

Sikhs must not think of the religious side of their life as being separate. Prayer, hard work and generosity are all equally important. Sikhs are discouraged from spending all their time on the religious aspects of life, such as prayer. They must live lives which are complete and contribute to the welfare of the community.

Kirat karna

Kirat karna means that Sikhs must earn their living honestly. Everyone has a responsibility to earn a living if they possibly can. It does not matter what the work is, provided that it is honest and not against the teachings of the Gurus. Therefore, a Sikh should never earn money from selling illegal drugs or doing something which might take advantage of other people.

Sikhism teaches that it is not wrong to be rich provided that the money is gained honestly, but that it is wrong to live your life just in order to make a lot of money. The money which a Sikh earns is used for his or her family and also for the **Khalsa** and the community as a whole.

A Sikh hospital in Nairobi

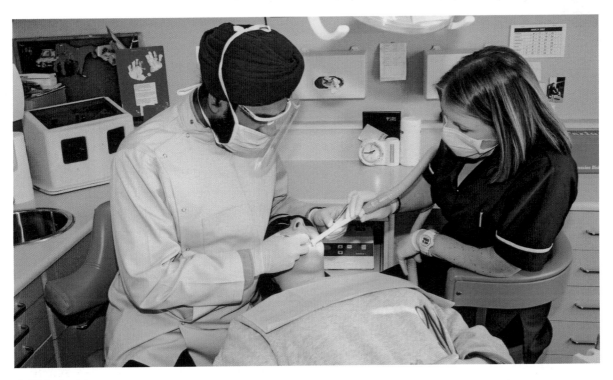

A Sikh dentist

Vand chhakna

Vand chhakna teaches Sikhs that they should live their lives on the principles of generosity and self-sacrifice.

Guru Amar Das Ji taught Sikhs the idea of **daswandh**. This means giving a tenth of spare money to the community. Money given in this way may be used for building schools or hospitals or to help those who are poor or suffering.

Three virtues

The first virtue for Sikhs is truth. 'Truthful living' is a life lived according to the example of the Gurus.

The second virtue is contentment. Someone who is contented is free from ambition, envy, greed and jealousy.

Patience gives people courage to put up with all the problems of everyday life.

Faith and compassion

The fourth virtue for Sikhs is perfect faith in the Gurus. Although Sikhs may feel that they are being tested, they must never lose faith or follow anyone except the Gurus.

The fifth virtue is compassion. This means looking at someone else's problem as your own, and doing everything you can to relieve it.

Women in Sikhism

In this section you will:

● learn about the Sikh attitude towards women

● learn why this is an important part of Sikh life and teaching.

Sikhism is one of the few religions where women have an equal role with men.

A Sikh woman can choose her own way of life, and many continue their education to university in order to fulfil their ambition for a professional career.

Where there is any suggestion that Sikhism is treating women differently from men, this is because of society and history and goes against the teachings of the **Gurus**.

Women can be members of the **Khalsa**, in exactly the same ceremony as men, and can become a **granthi**. The role of women in services in the **gurdwara** is increasing.

The reason why many women did not assist with Sikh ceremonies in the past was due to the general prejudices of the period rather than to any sexist belief.

We are God's own people, neither high nor low nor in between … Religion consists not in mere talk. He who looks on all alike and consider all to be equal is acclaimed as truly religious.

Guru Granth Sahib Ji

Guru Nanak Dev Ji taught that:

From women born, shaped in the womb, to woman betrothed and wed;
We are bound to women by ties of affection, on women man's future depends.
If one woman dies he seeks another; with a woman he orders his life.
Why then should one speak evil of women, they who give birth to kings?

Guru Granth Sahib Ji

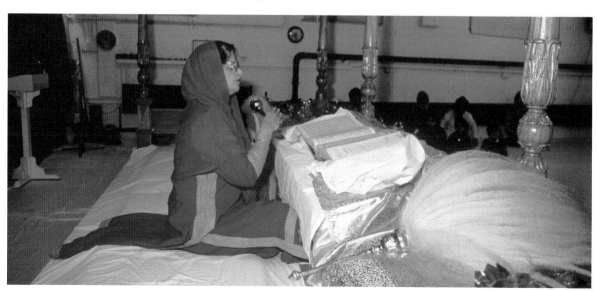

A women granthi leading the worship in the gurdwara

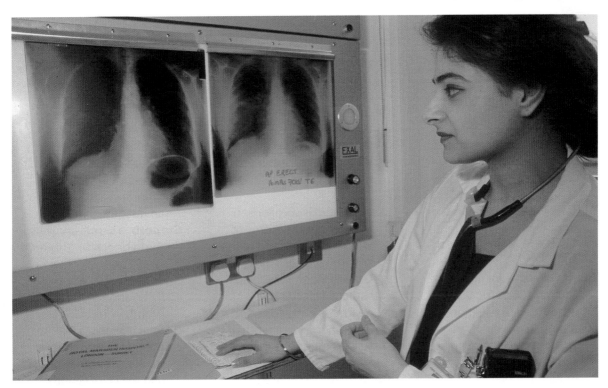

A Sikh doctor

The Gurus also taught that people should not follow the Hindu practice of giving dowries to a man in order to marry a particular woman. They also condemned suttee – the idea that when a man dies his wife should kill herself on his funeral pyre.

In the gurdwara

Men and women sit separately in the gurdwara. This is done so that no one touches the wife or husband of another person by accident. If more women than men are expected, then the women sit on the larger side.

The custom is that, normally, people sit on the side on which they sat on the first day the gurdwara was used.

Women granthis

Both men and women can perform the duties of a granthi in a gurdwara. There is no discrimination against any Sikh being a granthi. There are more male granthis than women because, particularly in a gurdwara where the granthi is a full-time job, a woman with children might find it difficult to carry out the duties. Sometimes, a husband and wife will share the duties of the granthi. The true equality of men and women is a very important aspect of Sikh life.

Glossary

Adi Granth a collection of the hymns of the first four Gurus and some of those of Guru Arjan Dev Ji

A hankar pride

Akal Takht 'Throne of the Eternal'. The building facing the Golden Temple in Amritsar

Akhand Path a continuous reading of the Guru Granth Sahib Ji from beginning to end

Amrit 'nectar'. Sanctified liquid made of sugar and water, used in initiation ceremonies

Amritsar a city in the Punjab and the location of the Golden Temple

Amritvela early morning prayer and meditation

Anand Sahib 'Hymn of bliss'

Anandpur Sahib a town in a valley at the foot of the Himalayas. The ashes of the head of Guru Tegh Bahadur Ji are buried there. It is also the place where Guru Gobind Singh Ji founded the Khalsa

Ardas the prayer offered during most religious acts

Asa di var the morning hymn

Baisakhi a major Sikh festival celebrating the foundation of the Khalsa in 1699

Belief accepting that something is true

Bhakti devotion to God, worship

Caste the Hindu belief that people are born into different social groups

Chanani a canopy over the scriptures, used as a mark of respect

Chauri a symbol of the authority of the Guru Granth Sahib Ji. A fin waved over scriptures, made of yak hair or nylon

Dasam Granth a collection of compositions, some of which are attributed to the tenth Sikh Guru, Guru Gobind Singh Ji, compiled some years after his death

Daswandh giving a tenth of surplus money to the community

Dhan material service to other people

Diwali Mela the festival which marks the end of the rainy season and the escape and return to Amritsar of Guru Har Gobind Ji

Diwan congregational worship

Faith believing or trusting in something

Five Ks see Panj kakke

Goindwal the location of a deep well or baoli built by Guru Amar Das Ji

Golak a long box in which worshippers place their offerings of money

Granthi a reader of the Guru Granth Sahib Ji, who officiates at ceremonies

Gurbani the word of God revealed by the Gurus. Also the Shabads, contained in the Guru Granth Sahib Ji

Gurdwara Sikh place of worship. Literally the 'doorway to the Guru'

Gurmukh someone who lives by the Gurus' teaching

Gurmukhi 'from the Guru's mouth'. The name given to the script in which the scriptures and the Punjabi language are written

Gurpurb a Guru's anniversary (birth or death). This term is also used for other anniversaries, e.g. the installation of the Adi Granth in 1604

Guru a teacher. In Sikhism, the title of Guru is used for the ten human Gurus and the Guru Granth Sahib Ji

Guru Granth Sahib Ji the Sikh scriptures, compiled by Guru Arjan Dev Ji and given its final form by Guru Gobind Singh Ji

Guru Nanak Dev Ji (1469–1539) the first Guru and the founder of the Sikh faith

Gutka a collection of Sikh hymns

Harimandir Sahib the Golden Temple in Amritsar

Hola Mohalla Mela the festival which celebrates Guru Gobind Singh Ji holding a three-day festival at Anandpur

Hukam 'God's will'

Ik Onkar 'There is only One God'. The first phrase of the Mool Mantar. It is also used as a symbol to decorate Sikh objects

Japji Sahib a morning prayer, composed by Guru Nanak Dev Ji, which forms the first chapter of the Guru Granth Sahib Ji

Kachera traditional underwear/shorts. One of the five Ks
Kam lust or desire
Kangha a comb worn in the hair. One of the five Ks
Kara a steel band, worn on the right wrist. One of the five Ks
Karah parshad sanctified food distributed at Sikh ceremonies
Karma actions and their consequences
Karodh anger
Kaur 'Princess'. Name given to all Sikh females
Kesh uncut hair. One of the five Ks
Khalsa 'The community of the pure'. The Sikh community
Khanda a double-edged sword used in the initiation ceremony. Also used as the emblem on the Sikh flag
Kirat karna earning one's livelihood by one's own efforts
Kirpan a sword. One of the five Ks
Kirtan devotional singing of the compositions found in the Guru Granth Sahib Ji
Kirtan Sohila a prayer said before going to sleep. It is also used at the cremation ceremony and when the Guru Granth Sahib Ji is laid to rest

Langar 'Guru's kitchen'. The gurdwara dining hall and the food served in it

Lavan four verses which are sung at a wedding ceremony
Lobh greed

Mala prayer beads
Man mental service
Manji the small platform on which the scripture is placed
Manmukh thinking about oneself first
Maya delusion, looking at the world and ignoring God
Mela 'fair'. Used of Sikh festivals which are not gurpurbs
Milna the ceremony which takes place before the wedding service
Moh being too attached to the world
Mool Mantar 'basic teaching'. The basic statement of belief at the beginning of the Guru Granth Sahib Ji
Mukti escape from rebirth

Nam Japna remembering the name of God
Nam Simran meditation on the divine name, using passages of scripture
Nishan Sahib the Sikh flag, flown at gurdwaras
Nit nem saying the specified daily prayers

Pakha a fan used by Sikhs walking with the Gurus, keeping them cool in the hot areas of the Punjab
Palanquin a special carriage
Panj kakke 'the five Ks'. The symbols of Sikhism worn by Sikhs
Panj piare 'the five beloved ones'. Those first initiated into the Khalsa and those who perform the rite today

Ragi a Sikh musician who sings compositions from the Guru Granth Sahib Ji
Reincarnation the belief that people are reborn after their death
Romalla a cloth on which the Guru Granth Sahib Ji is placed

Sadharan Path [to come]
Sadhsangat congregation or assembly of Sikhs
Sahaj-dhari 'seekers after God'. Sikhs who are not members of the Khalsa
Sahib term of respect
Serovar the pool around the Golden Temple in Amritsar
Sewa service directed at the sadhsangat and gurdwara, but also to humanity in general
Shabad a hymn from the Guru Granth Sahib Ji, the divine word
Sikhism the religion of the Sikhs
Singh 'Lion'. Name adopted by Sikh males
Sodar Rahiras the prayer said before the evening meal
Sukhmani the Hymn of Peace

Tan physical service
Trust having confidence in something
Turban head covering worn by many Sikhs

Vand chhakna sharing one's time, talents and earnings with the less fortunate

Waheguru 'Wonderful Lord'. A Sikh name for God

Yatras visits to places associated with the Gurus and Sikhism

Index